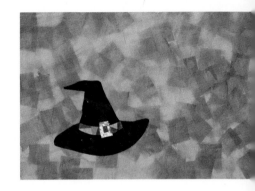

The Color Rap Book

by Ann Harris Smith

This book is dedicated to Big Annie and all those who helped her through her battle with ovarian cancer and continue to fight in her honor.

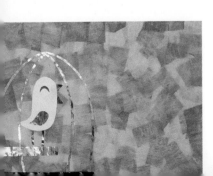

Red, red, red spells R-E-D

Pickin' cherries
from the cherry tree.

STOP

Red stop sign...

...and strawberries.

Red, red, red spells R-E-D

B-L-U-E

that spells

blue

Blueberry pie
for me and you.

Policeman's suit...

...and blue skies too.

B-L-U-E

that spells

blue

Yellow
is the color
of the
bright sunshine.

Ripe bananas...

...and corn sometimes

Yellow is the color of canary birds.

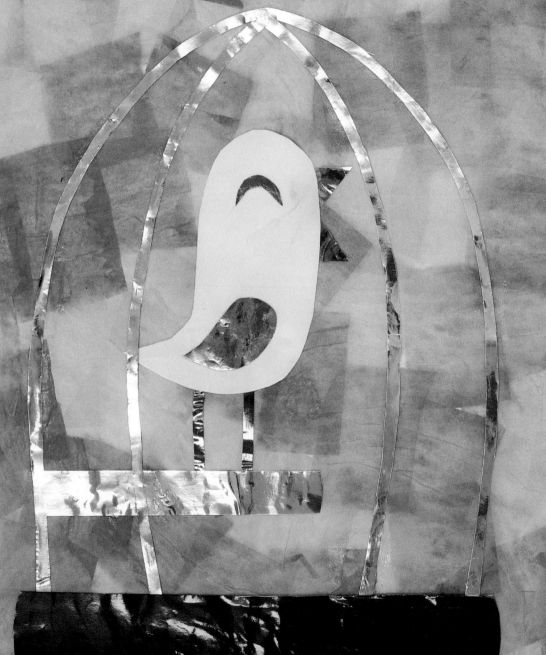

Now spell
yellow so you
can be heard.

Y-E-L-L-O-W

G-R-E-E-N

spells

green

Cutest frog you ever have seen.

Summer leaves...

...and summer grass.

Green, green light tells the cars they can pass.

O-R-A-N-G-E

Autumn leaves fall from the tree.

Jack o'lantern with a funny face.

Juicy oranges all over the place.

Purple is the color just for me

Grapes and jam...

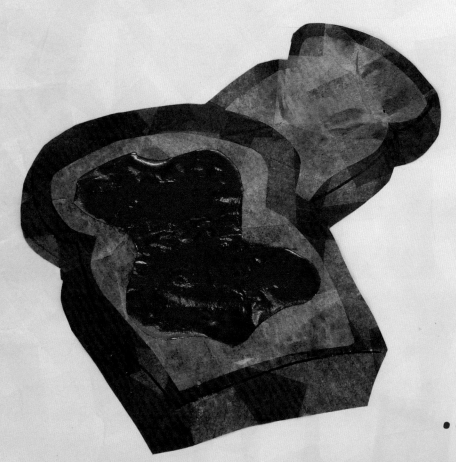

...and grape jelly.

P-U-R-P-L-E

Purple is the color just for me

B-R-O-W-N

spells

brown

Muddy water on the ground.

Brown, brown, brownies,

yum,

yum,

yum.

Chocolate bars for everyone.

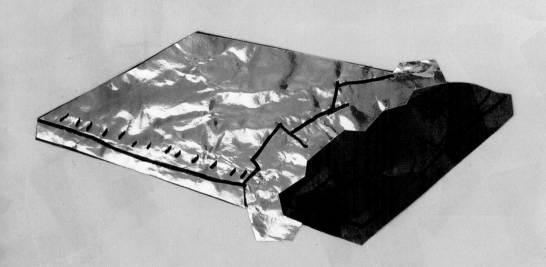

B-L-A-C-K

spells

black

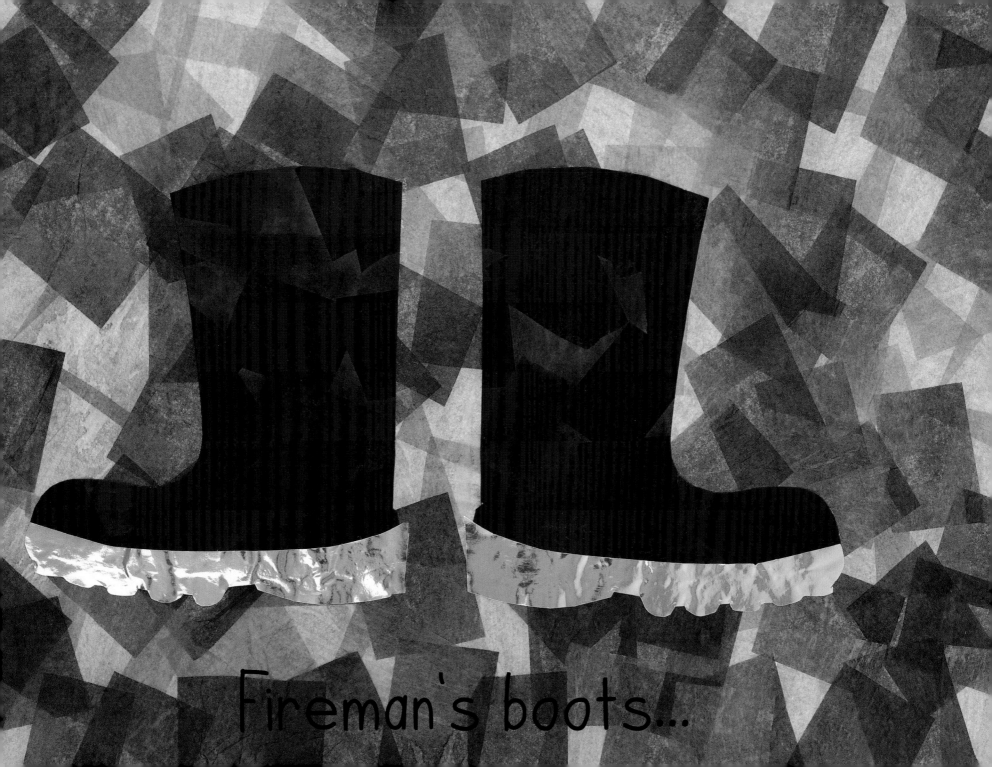

Fireman's boots...

...and a witch's hat.

Halloween bats

and Halloween cats.

B-L-A-C-K

spells

black

W-H-I-T-E

spells

white

White, white snow...

...and a bright, bright light.

Brides wear white...

...and ghosts do too.

Fluffy marshmallows for me and you.

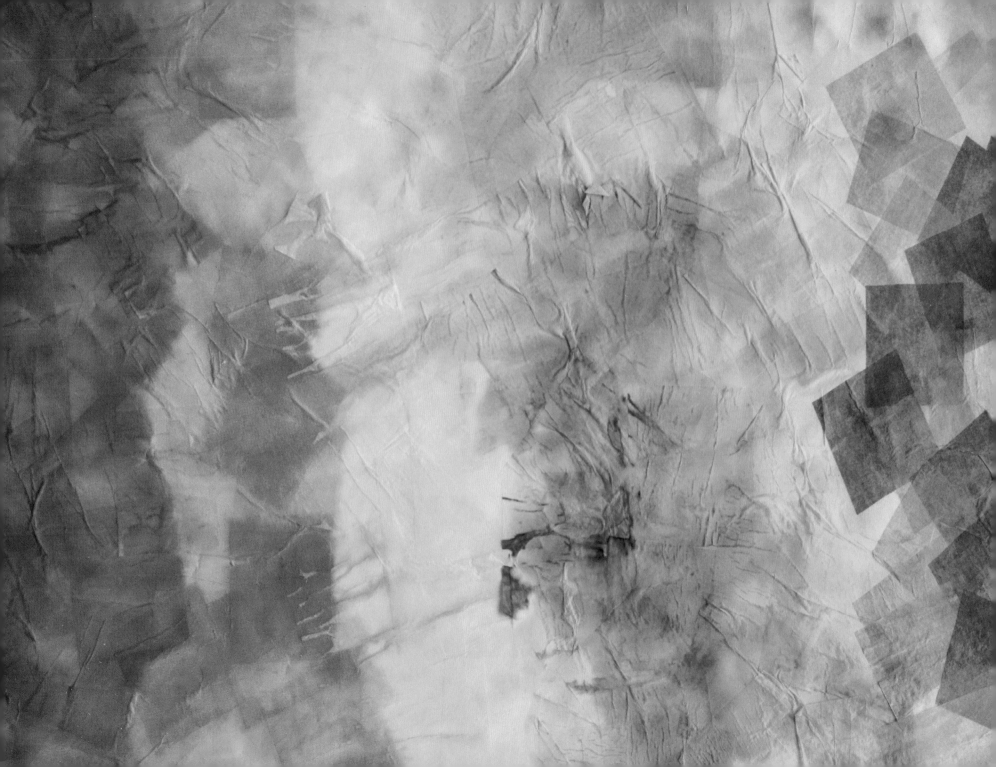

Ashley was in Ann's kindergarten class

Lauren Miller was not only a teaching colleague but a dear friend to Ann. For instance, they used to do aerobics in Lauren's basement when their children were little. Ann's daughter, Molly, babysat Lauren's daughters and now Lauren's youngest daughter, Ashley, often child-sits for Ann's grandchildren.

Lauren and Ann taught together in the same schools and the same grades. Ann used large visuals in her classroom to coordinate with the color raps. Lauren's daughter, Amber, created the art work used in the book in a way that they felt best represented what Ann would have used in her classroom. Ann also wore a special apron for her student's favorite learning activity, cooking! In these two pages, Lauren has offered us a few ingredients for a recipe that will be fun and educational for readers. They can all be used in different ways to supplement The Color Rap at home or in the classroom.

It is always a pleasure to hear stories from Lauren about Ann. Their friendship is everlasting and it shows.

We are truly grateful to Ashley, Lauren, & Amber for all of their love and effort in making The Color Rap Book come to life!

Ann loved teaching kindergarten and enjoyed making learning fun. It was also important to her that she reach all children at their level and their best mode of learning!

COLORING

ART PROJECTS

PAINTING

COOK THE COLORS

Try using:
Blueberry Pancakes for BLUE
Pumpkin Muffins for ORANGE
Dirt Dessert for BROWN
or Jello for any color!

When the book was printed for the very first time, we only printed a limited number.
This edition is a little bit different.
The content is the same, the artwork is the same, but we added something special.

The photo on the left is of Ashley Miller with Morgan Michael Smith, Ann's grandson. This picture was in the first print when Morgan was just 4 years old.

Now Morgan is 9 years old and a very talented artist!
The font used throughout the pages of the book was created by Morgan.
He is pictured here on the right and below, showing us his original concept.

MORGAN FONT!

Ann Harris Smith had a passion for early childhood education. She aspired to offer a loving and memorable year for the children and to spark a love of learning in them.

The Ann Harris Smith Foundation for Early Childhood Education made a special gift to the local school district where Ann taught Kindergarten.

Forward facing bookshelves were installed so that students can easily read the cover. Height appropriate tables and chairs were donated for students to use in the library.

The Color Raps were a tool that Ann created to bring rhymes together with colorful pictures and songs to help children learn all about colors. Ann was an avid runner and combined her love of teaching and running to create the color raps. Wanting to come up with a fun way to introduce colors, the rhythm of her feet hitting the ground provided the beat …red, red, red spelled R-E-D. As she introduced the color the children were also enveloped with her love of cooking. Goodies like blueberry pancakes, spaghetti sauce and sweet potato muffins were cooked and eaten. *Learning was fun and delicious!*

After a 2 year battle with ovarian cancer, Ann passed away in July 2002 at the age of 53. The Ann Harris Smith Foundation was created in 2000 by Ann and her family. Ovarian cancer awareness and early childhood education initiatives are the pillars of the foundation. Ann saw education as a tool to serve the greater good. She said, "If we can help just one person, we are going to make a difference." Her inherent altruism still defines our work, our approach and our mission; community-driven outreach that supports educational opportunities for our schools, our families, our workplaces, and our neighborhoods.

Ann's daughter Molly, shared one of her special memories about her mother as a teacher: "My Mom always was able to relate to young children and they gravitated towards her... it was an amazing thing to watch. She spent many years of her teaching life with Kindergarten children. She would always say that they came into her classroom as babies at the beginning of the year, but by the end, they were little people learning to read and soaking up so much knowledge like little sponges!"

Through the generosity of those who attend the Laurel Auto Group Pro-Am Charity Golf Tournament, the foundations' sole fund-raising event, support is provided to women and their families in our region who are affected by ovarian cancer, by raising awareness, and educating the community of the signs & symptoms of the disease.

Ann's legacy lives on in the lives of the students she taught throughout her career. The Color Rap Book enables Ann's legacy to continue through education in classrooms and to support our local community every year.

Matt and his son, Morgan, signing the Teal-mobile awareness vehicle at the annual Pro-Am.

The Smith family pictured above. Matt with wife, Tori, & their children, Ben, Cameron, & Morgan.

Pictured above are Ann's grandchildren, Ben, Cam, & Morgan. Big brother Ben enjoys reading to his brothers, Morgan & Cam.

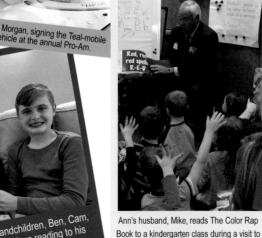

Ann's husband, Mike, reads The Color Rap Book to a kindergarten class during a visit to the local elementary school where Ann taught. The school still uses The Color Rap Book in their curriculum every year!

Pictured above are Ann's grandchildren, Anna and Noah, spending time together, having fun, & reading.

The Morris family pictured above. Molly husband, Tim, and their two children Anna and Noah.